ADVANCE PRAISE

"*It Takes a Village* is exactly what parents of exceptional children have been needing! As a professional working in the field for more than 10 years, I often find that following a diagnosis, many parents are not provided with the resources needed to obtain the best support for their child and family. Amy guides you through the journey of building a strong support system with actionable steps and relatability. What I love most is the fact that the book not only focuses on the child, but also on supporting the family as a unit. I will be recommending this book to all families I work with in the future."

- Jessica Andrews, M.A., BCBA - President/Owner of Take a Break Behavioral Babysitting

"*Parenting a disabled child often forces parents into the role of an advocate; which can be isolating and frightening. In* **It Takes a Village**... Amy provides parents and caregivers the foundational resources needed to find and maintain their own support system. The advocacy community will find Amy's book a helpful guide as they embark upon their own journeys."

- Aaron Wright, author of Thirteen Doors

"*It Takes a Village* is a must-read for all special needs families. As a single Dad to 3 amazing kids on the autism spectrum, I know how incredibly important my support system is and how incredibly lost I felt trying to put it together as a freshly minted special needs dad. Amy does a fantastic job of helping parents, both new and experienced, gain the insight and knowledge needed to build a supportive group of people around themselves, their child, and the rest of their family, who are there to help. I recommend this book to anyone coming to me for guidance, and I recommend it to you as well."

– Rob Gorski, The Autism Dad – Author, Advocate, Influencer

"It Takes a Village is the only book you'll need to start learning how to be the best parent for your child with exceptional needs. Not only does Amy help families build a support system, but she helps with all the complexities that go into this special parenting journey. A must-read!"

- Wendy Valente – Owner of Live Well Designs and Designing Interiors for Autism

"It Takes a Village provides an essential guide for the parents of children with exceptional needs and shines a bright light through the ever-winding labyrinth of community and familial supports that families can gather along the way throughout the journey of exceptional needs parenting."

- Shirleyann Kaigle – mother to two children, one with Autism Spectrum Disorder

"Whether you are a parent, a teacher, a professional, or a friend of the family; living with a loved one on the Spectrum is a blessing that requires support from all. This book will help inspire and guide all the members of the support team to make the journey of Autism and ADHD one of collaboration and love."

- Meegan Winters - Co-Founder, CEO of Able Eyes

IT TAKES A VILLAGE:

HOW TO BUILD A SUPPORT SYSTEM FOR YOUR EXCEPTIONAL NEEDS FAMILY

BY

AMY NIELSEN

AAPC PUBLISHING
PO Box 861116
Shawnee, KS 66218
Local Phone (913) 897-1004 Fax (913) 728-6090
www.aapcautismbooks.com
Copyright © 2021 by Amy Nielsen
Printed in the United States of America

Published June 2021 by AAPC Publishing

Names: Nielsen, Amy, author.
Title: It takes a village : how to build a support system for your exceptional needs family / by Amy Nielsen.
Description: Shawnee, KS : AAPC Publishing, [2021] | Includes bibliographical references and index.
Identifiers: ISBN: 978-1-942197-71-3 (paperback) | 978-1-942197-72-0 (ebook)
Subjects: LCSH: Parents of exceptional children--Handbooks, manuals, etc. | Parents of developmentally disabled children--Handbooks, manuals, etc. | Parents of autistic children--Handbooks, manuals, etc. | Parents of attention-deficit-disordered children--Handbooks, manuals, etc. | Social networks--Handbooks, manuals, etc. | Exceptional children--Family relationships. | Developmentally disabled children--Family relationships. | Children with autism spectrum disorders--Family relationships. | Attention-deficit-disordered children-- Family relationships. | Hyperactive children--Family relationships. | BISAC: FAMILY & RELATIONSHIPS / Autism Spectrum Disorders. | FAMILY & RELATIONSHIPS / Attention Deficit Disorder (ADD-ADHD) | FAMILY & RELATIONSHIPS / Children with Special Needs. | REFERENCE / Personal & Practical Guides. | LITERARY COLLECTIONS / Diaries & Journals. Classification: LCC: HQ759.913 .N54 2021 | DDC: 649/.1526--dc23

AAPC PUBLISHING
Your First Source for Practical Solutions for Autism Spectrum and Related Disorders
Exceptional Resources For Extraordinary Minds

This book is a guide to help families of
children with developmental disabilities,
such as ADHD and Autism Spectrum Disorder,
build a support system for themselves,
their children, and their entire family.

TABLE OF CONTENTS

Dedication

I dedicate this book to my village.

INTRODUCTION

Having a support system is like having
a safety net below you at all times.
— Author Unknown

Exhausted? Afraid? Overwhelmed? You are not alone. Raising a child with an exceptional need, such as Attention Deficit Hyperactivity Disorder (ADHD) or Autism Spectrum Disorder (ASD), is undeniably demanding. Parents and caregivers often feel overpowered and under-supported. They need all the help they can get. I know this because I am one of them.

My youngest son is six years old. He has ADHD and ASD. His older siblings were in their teens and twenties by the time he was born. Even though parenting a special needs child was new to me, I was confident I could handle this on my own. I thought my 20 plus years of experience as a parent and educator prepared me for the task. I was so wrong.

The demands of this parenting role are unique, and to parent the most effectively requires a support system or your village, as I like to call it. It helps if you fill your village with people who are as passionate about helping your child as you are, people you trust, and who are willing to help.

Building your village will include individual and specific goals because every family's support system will look different. Some families have nearby grandparents who are always available; some don't. Some parents are on this journey without a spouse or partner. Some families live in rural areas that may have little to no access to services. Regardless of your circumstances, you still can and should build a village of support for yourself and your family.

This guide will identify seven distinct areas of your village, stress the importance of each, and offer tips on building each one. At the end of each chapter, there is a section for you to review the information you have learned, and to express your own thoughts. You will define what the seven areas look like for you now, create goals to strengthen them, and then reflect on the process.

Now it's time to get your hands dirty and build your village from the ground up. Let's go!

1

MY VILLAGE INCLUDES ME

Without a solid foundation,
you'll have trouble creating anything of value.
– Erika Oppenheimer

You are the foundation of your village. Therefore, before you look outward, you may want to look inward. Self-care is what I am talking about here.

Self-care is important for everyone, but for parents of children with exceptional needs, it takes on a whole new meaning. We are more likely to suffer from depression, anxiety, extreme weight gain, extreme weight loss, poor nutrition, illness, disease, and have relationship problems than parents of children who don't have special needs.

Parents and caregivers of special needs children frequently report they don't have the time or the energy for self-care. They also report battling feelings of guilt for addressing their own needs when their children's needs are so great.

However, not taking care of yourself depletes you of the energy required to manage the stressful demands of parenting your exceptional child. It's a vicious cycle that, if not intentionally addressed, can impact your entire family.

Self-care is not selfish. It is selfless. When you care for yourself as well as possible, you will be the best parent possible.

This chapter will explain the importance of and give suggestions to improving self-care for your physical, emotional, intellectual, social, and spiritual health.

PHYSICAL HEALTH

Your physical health is the condition of your brain and your body. Of course, we don't have control over our age, illness, and disease. However, most of us have some control over our physical activity level, nutrition, and how much sleep we get.

PHYSICAL ACTIVITY

For optimal brain and body health, physical activity is vital. It is important, not only to build muscles or fitness (although those are important), but to feel calmer, have more energy, and improve your sense of well-being. As parents of special needs children, it is often difficult for us to carve out time for physical activities that don't pertain to our child. But just a few minutes a day can make a huge impact, even if that few minutes a day is while you are doing something else!

Fitness and nutritional expert Bethanne Weiss says to start by making small, simple tweaks in your daily routines, such as walking your cart back to the grocery store entrance or taking the stairs instead of an elevator. If you are within walking distance of shops, hit the pavement instead of drive. Turn on music and dance with your kids.

One simple way I add movement into my daily routine is while brewing my morning cup of coffee. As the Keurig is doing its job, I drop to the floor and do a few pushups or planks. Next, I do walking lunges and squats around my kitchen. Rather than spending that time staring at the Keurig, I use it to sneak in a few extra minutes of physical activity.

In addition to the physical benefits, physical activity awakens our brain and releases endorphins which help us feel good. You don't need to spend an hour at the gym or take a run (although those are great forms of physical activity) to get that benefit. Rethinking your already-in-place everyday habits and routines is an easy first step.

NUTRITION

Equally as important as your level of physical activity for your overall health is your diet. Most of what you eat should be nutritionally dense foods. These are foods that are low in calories and high in nutrients, such as fruits and vegetables, whole grains, low-fat dairy products, seafood, lean meats, eggs, peas, beans, and nuts.

Eating healthy can be challenging for parents of exceptional needs children because sensory sensitivities and restricted eating patterns can impact our kids' food preferences. Preparing two separate meals at the end of a demanding day may not be possible. One way to help is to prepare either their meals or yours ahead of time. Also, have fresh fruits and veggies washed and ready for snacking to help you resist the urge to reach for unhealthy comfort foods.

But most importantly, rather than worrying about what you shouldn't eat, shift your mindset to what you should eat. Adding more nutritionally dense foods to your current diet is a great start.

An excellent resource to learn how to make small swaps to improve your physical health is Bethanne Weiss' book *Move Your Assets: From the Chair, Not the Bank*. Bethanne has more than 30 years of experience in what she calls "moving assets." With a humorous approach, she offers easy-to-follow tips and suggestions for getting healthy. Her tips are fun, simple to implement, and most importantly, provide outstanding results.

Bethanne helps caregivers that have little to no time for self-care find ways to work it into their already busy days by focusing on small swaps to existing daily routines.

ADEQUATE SLEEP

Being the parent or caregiver of a child with a developmental disability is exhausting, and studies show this group doesn't regularly get the recommended 7-8 hours of sleep per night.

According to a study in the Journal of Pediatric Psychology, "Parents of children with ASD reported poorer sleep quality than the TD (typically developing) group. Also, parents of children with ASD had objectively different sleep patterns, with an earlier wake time and shorter sleep time than parents of TD children" (Meltzer, 2008, p. 380).

In addition to their child's sleep patterns, other contributing factors can impact these parents' sleep. Daily tasks may be tough to keep up with when their child is awake. Therefore, they may use their child's sleep time to catch up on responsibilities. Sometimes, these parents may stay awake after their child is asleep to have valuable downtime or reconnect with their partner. But the research is clear; a lack of adequate sleep can have severe consequences.

According to an article on Healthline, inadequate sleep can affect your memory, cause difficulty with thinking and concentration, affect your mood, increase your risk of car and other accidents, weaken your immune system, increase your risk of high blood pressure, increase your risk of weight gain, increase your risk of diabetes, decrease your sex drive, increase your risk of heart disease, and impact your balance and coordination (Watson, 2019).

So how can you make time for more sleep when it seems as if you barely have enough hours in the day to get everything done? Here are a few tips!

Set a bedtime.

Without a bedtime, it is easy to get into a habit of falling asleep on the couch while trying to watch one more episode of your favorite show. Setting a bedtime will train your body to want to sleep at that time, causing you to have a good night's rest and wake up refreshed and energized.

Follow a bedtime routine.

If you are the parent of a child with ASD, you certainly understand the value of routines! Your child probably has a specific evening routine they follow that helps them wind down and prepare for sleep. Create an evening routine for yourself, such as having a warm bath followed by reading a chapter of a book or writing in a journal. What works for your child can work for you!

Avoid screens.

Screens can affect your ability to get proper sleep. Watching television or checking emails on your phone keeps you alert. Also, the blue light emitted from a screen can alter your body's ability to secrete melatonin. Melatonin is a hormone that controls your sleeping and waking cycle, otherwise known as the circadian rhythm. Most experts recommend no screens for at least 30 minutes before bed (SCLHealth.org, n.d.).

Your sleeping environment should be comfortable and conducive to good sleep.

For me, clean and fresh-smelling sheets, white noise, a soft night light, a body pillow, a cool room, and cozy pajamas help me settle in for the night. Define what a comfortable sleep environment looks and feels like for you, and create it. You'll look forward to climbing into your bed each night.

EMOTIONAL HEALTH

Emotional health is the ability to be in control of your thoughts, feelings, and behaviors. Emotionally healthy people are aware and in charge of their emotions. They can cope with everyday stress and responsibilities. They have good self-esteem and healthy relationships with others.

Due to the demanding mental and physical strain of being a parent of a child with exceptional needs, there is a huge possibility that your emotional health may suffer.

When my son was first diagnosed with autism, I went through a rough period. I think most parents do. One day I abruptly ended relationships with friends whose children were my son's same age but did not have autism. Hearing all the milestones my friends' children were reaching that my son wasn't reaching discouraged me. I explained this to them, and although they were disappointed, they understood.

I knew this was not emotionally healthy, so I acted. I found a therapist who specialized in working with families of children with autism. She helped me work through what I was feeling and taught me effective coping strategies. After about six months of therapy, I was able to rekindle those friendships.

Additionally, my therapist told me that I needed a support system. I needed to put together a team of friends, family, and experts to offer my family and me the support we needed to regain our footing as a cohesive family unit. She taught me to accept our new norm, embrace our son's truth, develop a new healthier outlook, let go of my expectations, and embrace the life we had, not the one I thought we would have. This book is the outcome of that time spent with her.

According to a recent article on Healthline.com:

> Good emotional health is crucial to your overall well-being. If you feel like your thoughts and emotions are getting the best of you, taking care of your core needs — like sleep and connection with loved ones — can help. If that doesn't seem to do the trick, consider working with a therapist or another mental health professional. They can help you identify the aspects of your emotional health you want to improve and help you come up with a plan. (Lamothe, 2019)

How do you know if you are emotionally healthy? If you are happier more often than you are sad, then chances are you have balanced emotional health. But to be more specific, analyze these three areas of your life: your thoughts, feelings, and behaviors. Are all three in alignment? You can focus your time and energy (your behaviors) on positive things such as taking care of yourself and your child and still have negative thoughts and feelings. We all have our bad days, but if you currently have more bad days than good, it may be time to seek professional help.

I am eternally grateful for the professional help I received early in my son's diagnosis and my exceptional needs parenting journey. I truly believe it contributed to my optimistic outlook on our family. I never want to diminish how difficult raising a child with exceptional needs can be, but I wholeheartedly believe that while there are things out of our control, what is in our control is our mindset. Sometimes, a little professional support is all we need to help us realize that and come to terms with the life we have, the child we have, and the joy in this journey.

Intellectual Health

Intellectual health is using your brain in creative, stimulating, and knowledge-seeking activities. Ali Geary from Illinois State University writes, "It is important to gain and maintain intellectual wellness because it expands knowledge and skills in order to live a stimulating and successful life." She then gives suggestions for activities to stimulate your intellectual health, such as reading for pleasure or playing a board game (Geary, 2014).

Intellectual health is significant in my life. When I don't challenge myself intellectually through learning something new or being creative, I become lethargic and unmotivated.

As special needs parents, we are always busy! Try these suggestions for simple yet effective ways to boost your intellectual health. And, like me, maybe you'll feel energized and rejuvenated!

Read

There is a reason teachers frequently give their students reading assignments. Reading is a fantastic way to boost your intellectual health. Read both for pleasure and to learn about topics that interest you. If you don't have the time to cozy up with your favorite book, try listening to audio versions.

Watch documentaries

Documentaries are non-fiction movies created to educate and provide new and exciting angles on a wide range of real-world topics and stories. They can be fascinating and highly entertaining, and you will learn something new!

One thing to keep in mind is that documentaries cover a wide variety of topics. It may be a good idea to choose positive and uplifting episodes. Then when you turn the television off, you feel uplifted yourself!

Keep a journal

Writing down what is going on in your life is an excellent exercise for your brain. It is information recall, but it can help you analyze and solve problems more efficiently. Journaling is also a great stress reducer and allows you a safe place to record your feelings.

Consider journaling first thing in the morning as a way to plan your day and record your thoughts and expectations. Journaling last thing in the evening helps your mind dump all the thousands of thoughts that may have accumulated in your brain during the day. You can then let those go, and hopefully, that can pave the way for a good night's sleep.

Play games

Challenging board games, crosswords, sudoku puzzles, and similar activities are not only fun to play but also stimulate your brain.

You can find board games simple enough to play with your children, challenging enough to play with a friend or partner, and solo games for when you are alone. Board games are one of the best low-tech entertainment and brain-boosting activities you can choose, and they are fun!

The Arts

Attending a play, listening to music, creating something beautiful on canvas, clay, or with yarn, or learning to play (or rediscover) an instrument are all things that open you up to new experiences, and these new experiences have intellectual benefits.

And it is never too late to learn (or rediscover)! Today, especially with thousands of "How-To" videos readily available online (many free of charge), you can learn (or have fun trying) a variety of new things.

Meaningful conversations

Conversations about engaging topics with other people can help stimulate you mentally and serve as a strategy to help you maintain and even build upon your intellectual health.

Engaging in activities like these that stimulate your brain will improve your overall health and happiness.

SOCIAL HEALTH

Social health is your ability to create and maintain meaningful relationships. People are social beings, and a lack of social interaction and meaningful relationships can lead to obesity, depression, high blood pressure, and disease. I will address in more detail the importance of meaningful relationships with friends in Chapter Four. For this section, the focus is on the significance of time devoted to interaction with people outside of your family.

According to an article by Jane E. Brody of the New York Times, "People who are chronically lacking in social contacts are more likely to experience elevated levels of stress and inflammation. These, in turn, can undermine the well-being of nearly every bodily system, including the brain." She states that a lack of social interaction is as unhealthy for our bodies as obesity, smoking, and a lack of exercise (Brody, 2017).

Research shows socializing is essential for our health and well-being. Parents of children with developmental disabilities often suffer socially. They may withdraw from social settings for several reasons, such as inadequate childcare or the stress of anticipating how their child may react in a particular environment.

For the first two years of my son's autism diagnosis, I felt like I was on lockdown (and this was long before the pandemic). After my son suffered multiple meltdowns and other challenging behaviors in places such as birthday parties, theme parks, and friends' homes, I just thought, *I am done.* The stress I went through from worrying about what might happen was too much to endure. And while placing our social life on pause was isolating, it was also time to rethink what our social life could look like in the future.

Eventually, my son gained skills through behavior therapy, and our family learned to adapt to our new norm. We learned to adjust, and social settings became more successful. While I sometimes feel like I am holding my breath, just waiting for something to go wrong, there is a difference now. That difference is that we now have specific strategies to reduce and minimize potential problems when we are in social settings with our son.

When we do things outside of our home as a family, we are more careful with planning. The timing must fit within his nap and sleep schedule. We bring the food he will eat. My husband and I typically tag team in ten-minute shifts so that one of us is watching our son closely at all times. My son elopes, so we avoid outdoor activities in locations without gates or fences. We also avoid outdoor places with open bodies of water. We have figured out events we can attend and the ones we have to decline. Finally, we again have a social life; it just looks different than before.

Caregivers and parents of children with exceptional needs may find a social life challenging to maintain. Nonetheless, it still may be possible. You just might need to redefine your new norm, just like my family did. Create new guidelines. Learn to confidently say no when you don't think your child can cope, despite protests from family or friends. But then go on to create scenarios where you can say yes. Maybe that means hosting more events in your own home. Perhaps that means tag-teaming like my husband and I do. Maybe that means hiring a sitter so you can attend a social event.

If you have had difficulty hiring a sitter that has the specific abilities to effectively look after your child, try contacting a company that offers skilled respite care such as "Take a Break Babysitting Service." Owned by Board Certified Behavior Analyst Jessica Andrews, Take a Break contracts with Speech-Language Pathologists, Special Education Teachers, Registered Behavior Technicians, and other specialists across the country to help families find reliable babysitters.

If you aren't able or interested at this time in in-person social settings, there are so many online options via social media. By thoughtfully planning strategies and adapting, you can work toward building a fulfilling social life!

SPIRITUAL HEALTH

By spiritual health, I mean getting in touch with yourself on a deeper level and feeling connected with the universe; for some people, that may be a religious service or prayer. For others, that might be meditation, yoga, or journaling.

According to an article on spirituality in Psychology Today, higher spirituality levels have been linked to increased compassion, strengthened relationships, and improved self-esteem. (Psychology Today, n.d.) As parents of special needs children, I believe we need these in abundance!

Personally, immersing myself in water is where I experience spirituality. Whether floating in a swimming pool or a hot bathtub, the soothing feel of water relaxes me. I feel the most connected with myself and the most grateful for my blessings. To me, water represents the opposite of a finite and busy life; it's infinite and intentional space.

Here are some simple things you can do to strengthen your spiritual health:

Spend time in nature

Unplug from your devices and go outside. Fresh air, sunshine, and all the sights and smells of nature can instantly lift your mood. Incorporate as much time outdoors as possible. If all your schedule allows is a 10-minute walk around a lake at lunch, take it.

Do things for others

As busy parents of a child with exceptional needs, you might feel like you don't have the energy or the time to do for your own family, much less to do things for others. But doing things for others can be as simple as a phone call to a friend who's sick or letting someone ahead of you in a grocery line who has fewer items than you. Simple acts of kindness will boost your mood and help you feel a deeper connection with the universe.

Spend time alone

Even if it's just a few minutes a day, alone time is valuable. Whether it's a quiet bath, a walk, a morning meditation, or journaling, make time to be with yourself and your thoughts. During this time, be intentional about focusing on the positive things in your life and not on trying to solve the negatives.

MAKE IT PERSONAL

Self-care was the topic of Chapter 1. Why? Because it is that important! Remember, you cannot give what you do not have. It will help you fill your exceptional family's big needs if you fill your big needs first!

Here you can explore your current self-care level and set simple, realistic, and achievable goals for improvement!

Fill out this chapter's "Make it Personal," date it, and put a note on your calendar to come back and reflect on your progress in one month.*

Today's Date:_____

One Month Later:_____

Physical Activity

Has your physical activity changed since becoming the caregiver or parent of a child with exceptional needs? Do you feel you now have less time or are too exhausted to be physically active?

Can you think of ways to incorporate physical activity with your child?

Referring back to this chapter's simple suggestions, what are three easy ways to incorporate physical activity into your existing daily routines?

1. _____
2. _____
3. _____

Reflection: Has my physical activity improved over the previous month? Why or why not?

Nutrition

Have your eating habits changed since becoming the caregiver or parent of a child with exceptional needs? Do you find it more difficult to find the time or energy to cook healthy meals?

Referring back to this chapter's simple suggestions, what are three easy ways to incorporate more nutritionally dense foods into your existing diet?

1. _____
2. _____
3. _____

Reflection: Has my nutrition improved over the previous month? Why or why not?

Sleep

Have your sleep routines and the amount of sleep you get each night changed since becoming the caregiver or parent of a child with exceptional needs? If so, what do you think are contributing factors?

Referring back to this chapter's simple suggestions, what are three easy changes you can make to improve your sleep routine?

1. _____
2. _____
3. _____

Reflection: Has my sleep improved over the previous month? Why or why not?

Emotional Health

Has your emotional health been impacted since becoming a caregiver or parent of a child with exceptional needs? If so, in what ways?

Referring back to this chapter's simple suggestions, what are three easy ways to improve your emotional health? *(Please seek professional help if you are having more bad days than good.)*

1. _____
2. _____
3. _____

Reflection: Has my emotional health improved or declined over the last month? Why or why not?

Intellectual Health

Has your intellectual health been impacted since becoming the caregiver or parent of a child with exceptional needs? In which ways?

Referring back to this chapter's simple suggestions, what are three easy ways to improve your intellectual health?

1. _____
2. _____
3. _____

Reflection: Has my intellectual health improved over the last month? Why or why not?

Social Health

Describe your social health before becoming a parent or caregiver to a child with exceptional needs. How does that compare to today?

Referring back to this chapter's simple suggestions, what are three easy ways to improve your social health?

1. _____
2. _____
3. _____

Reflection: Has my social health improved over the last month? Why or why not?

Spiritual Health

Is spiritual health important to you? If so, describe what that looked like before having a child with exceptional needs versus today? Are there some things you'd like to change?

Referring back to this chapter's simple suggestions, what are three easy ways to improve your spiritual health?

1. _____
2. _____
3. _____

Reflection: How has my spiritual health improved over the last month?

*Please give yourself as much space as you need. Parenting an exceptional child isn't easy. If you find that not much has changed after your first month, that is okay! You are doing the best you can! You can always try again next month!

2

MY VILLAGE INCLUDES MY HOME

In essence, tidying ought to be the act of restoring balance among people, their possessions, and the house they live in.
– Marie Kondo

Families of children with exceptional needs often spend a great deal of time looking for resources outside the home, and understandably so. But how your home is organized and functions will impact your exceptional needs child and your entire family.

Home is where most families spend the majority of their time. It is where children learn how the world is supposed to function and their role in it. It should be a place of refuge, calm, and peace.

The good news: This is an area where families often have the most control. Optimizing your home environment isn't dependent on finances or outside resources, although I realize those can have an impact. Nonetheless, with nothing more than some thoughtful planning, families can work toward creating a happy and healthy home environment.

Your family will thrive in a home that is organized and runs smoothly. A cluttered, disorganized, and messy living space can undo all the hard work you are mentally and emotionally investing in building your village. Your home should feel like your sanctuary, a retreat from the outside world.

As a former children's librarian, I frequently read a book to my students called *Sally's Room* by Mary K. Brown. The main character, Sally, keeps a very messy room. When you first meet Sally at the beginning of the book, she is upset because she can't find what she needs for school that day. Toys litter her floor, and she steps on a small dinosaur injuring her foot. Before she leaves her house to go to school, she is already in a bad mood.

After she leaves for school, her bedroom clutter has a discussion, and they've had enough! The clutter follows Sally to school to confront her and demand she tidy her room. When she sees her bedroom clutter outside her classroom door, Sally is shocked.

As soon as the school bell rings, she quickly runs home, hoping to beat the clutter. She flings open her bedroom door to what is now an empty bedroom, and she is surprised at how big her room looks. She has space to dance and move around. Later, when the clutter returns, Sally is inspired to organize and tidy her room (Brown, 1992).

The message in the story is one I can relate to. When I was teaching full time, and my older three children were attending school, the clutter would take on a life of its own. Busy mornings meant there wasn't time to wash breakfast dishes or pick up pajamas. The end of the day brought afternoon clutter, stacks of homework papers, mail, dropped backpacks, and dirty lunchboxes. The AM and PM mess were in addition to existing loads of dirty laundry that needed washing and loads of clean laundry that needed folding. I bet you can relate.

Physical clutter can become mental clutter. It can hinder your ability to be productive at work, at home, and especially your ability to handle the demands of exceptional needs parenting.

Psychology Today shared a recent study by Susan Whitbourne at the University of Mexico that identified five areas in a person's life that a cluttered and disorganized home can impact.

1. ***Low subjective well-being***

   Clutter and messiness can prevent a person from seeing their home as a refuge or place of peace and cause them to feel their home is their enemy.

2. ***Unhealthy eating***

   A cluttered home can cause stress, and stress can lead to binge eating.

3. ***Poor mental health***

   Poor mental health can lead to depression and anxiety.

4. ***Less efficient visual processing***

   A disorganized home can inhibit your ability to read the emotions of others.

5. ***Less efficient thinking***

   Physical clutter can create mental clutter. Mental clutter can affect short-term memory tasks, long-term memory tasks and affect your ability to function efficiently and productively (Susan Whitbourne, 2017).

If you are reading this in your home, stop and look around. If you are in the kitchen, are the counters cluttered? Are there dirty dishes in the sink? When was the last time you cleaned out the refrigerator?

If you are in the living room, is it littered with toys and stacks of books or magazines? If you are in your bedroom, is the bed made? Is there a basket of laundry waiting to be folded and put away?

Visualize the condition of your closets, cabinets, and dresser drawers. Are they overflowing with clothes and things you don't need or use anymore? When you think about your home's overall condition, does the space make you feel peaceful or anxious? The answers to these questions matter. A cluttered and disorganized home will clutter and disorganize your mind.

If you feel overwhelmed by the amount of work you need to do to declutter and organize, it is understandable! Families of children with exceptional needs often don't have hours of available time or energy to start massive projects. But help is on the way! Here are some books and websites to provide you with suggestions and support.

1. *Allie Casazza: Declutter Like a Mother*
   www.alliecasazza.com

Allie's program emerged from her desire to get out from underneath her cluttered and chaotic life and then help others do the same. Allie encourages you to use her three-step process.

1. Declutter your home to reduce stress and create space for what matters.
2. Simplify your life by removing hidden and unnecessary burdens and taking better care of yourself.
3. Structure your day by creating rhythms and routines.

Her online courses, support groups, videos, blogs, and podcast episodes can help you declutter and put your home and even your life in order so you don't get overwhelmed.

I participated in her free "Declutter Like a Mother" 30-day challenge with great success. It was fun, engaging, and productive. She takes you step-by-step through the process of decluttering using encouraging and informative emails, live Facebook videos, and an online support group. She is the first person I recommend to anyone ready to rid their lives and homes of clutter and live a happier and more purposeful life (Casazza, 2017).

2. *Marie Kondo: The Life-Changing Magic of Tidying Up*
www.konmari.com

Marie Kondo is one of the newest influencers to revolutionize the home decluttering and organizational process. She teaches how to declutter by focusing on items that "spark joy." If an item in your home doesn't spark joy, you pass it on to someone in whose home it will. Her method uses this six-rule process:

1. Commit to tidy up.
2. Imagine your ideal lifestyle.
3. Discard first.
4. Tidy by category, not by location.
5. Follow the proper order.
6. Ask yourself if the item sparks joy.

Her New York Times bestseller, *The Life-Changing Magic of Tidying Up*, is a must-read. But that's just a start. She also offers unique organizing techniques, including a product line of tools to help you maximize space. Her website is full of helpful information, such as blog posts, videos, a newsletter sign-up, and more. I let go of more clutter than I expected using her program, and you can too (Kondo, 2014).

3. *Wendy Valente: Designing Interiors for Autism*
www.livewelldesigns.net

Once you've cleared the clutter and organized what's left, a great next step is to create an environment specifically designed to help your exceptional needs family thrive!

Interior designer Wendy Valente, also the mother of a child with autism, noticed sensory spaces popping up in commercial locations but couldn't find resources to craft similar spaces for her clients at the residential level. Seeing a need, she combined her love for interior design and passion for helping families like her own to fill that gap.

Within her business, *Live Well Designs*, she established *Designing Interiors for Autism*. Wendy helps families of children with autism and related disorders create personalized sensory spaces, bedrooms conducive to good sleep and relaxation, and shared family spaces that work for everyone.

Wendy says, "It's about you learning all the things that make your child unique and facilitating their needs with the perfect item, understanding how color, clutter, lighting, textures, and layout all play an important role in creating a space exactly for the activity and the person using the space."

MAKE IT PERSONAL

Optimizing your home environment was the topic of Chapter 2. Why? Because creating a home that is a place of refuge and peace will help your exceptional needs family thrive!

Fill out this chapter's "Make it Personal," date it, and put a note on your calendar to come back and *reflect on your progress in one month.

Today's Date:_____

One Month Later:_____

My Home

Does your home feel neat and tidy or cluttered and disorganized?

Did you grow up in a home that was neat and tidy or cluttered and disorganized? Do you feel that contributed to the way you run your home?

Would you like to make some improvements to optimize your home environment for you and your family? If so, what specifically would you like to improve?

Referring back to this chapter's simple suggestions, what are three easy ways to improve your home's environment?

1. _____
2. _____
3. _____

Reflection: Have I made improvements to my home's environment over the last month? If so, what were those improvements?

If not, I am going to let it go and try again next month.

3

MY VILLAGE INCLUDES
MY FAMILY

Family is your most reliable source of support in any situation
because love from your family is unconditional.
– Oscar Auliq-Ice

While it is essential to take care of yourself and your home to meet the demands of exceptional needs parenting, other people are what will make your village thrive.

Raising a special needs child is demanding. It is nearly impossible to carry out the multitude of essential responsibilities if you shoulder them alone, and you don't have to. The first people you should reach out to are your family. Remember, they love you and your child unconditionally. They want to help you.

However, parents of special needs children are sometimes reluctant to reach out to their families. Perhaps they fear their child may be a burden. Deep down, they may wish and hope that their family would offer assistance.

But the reality is that your family may not know how to help, if their help is needed, or if you trust them to help – especially if you haven't asked. So how can you receive the support that you desperately need from your family? The following suggestions may help.

Ask for specific help.

Your family may not realize how they can help, so tell them. If you have able family members, ask one to take your child to school or pick them up a few days a week to give you time to catch up on errands. Ask a family member to babysit your child for a few hours a week so you can visit a friend or attend a fitness class. By being specific about what you need, you are more likely to get support.

What if my family can't look after my child?

If you don't have family close by or who are capable of looking after your child, they can still be an essential part of your support system. Although they would help if they could, my husband's family lives in another country. My family lives nearby, but I can't expect them to look after my son. His needs and abilities are unique, and someone without an in-depth knowledge of autism and ADHD can't step in. Perhaps you feel the same.

Nonetheless, our families are still a significant part of my village. I call them regularly and tell them what is going on in my son's life, the good, the bad, and the ugly. They are my shoulder to lean on when things get overwhelming, and they are there with the attaboy when we achieve success.

Despite my mother not being able to look after my son alone, there are other ways she offers her support. When my husband has to travel, she spends the night. In the mornings, she gets my son dressed for school and entertains him. This allows me to get his lunch packed and get myself ready for the day.

When my older children were younger, a relative and I worked out an arrangement. She'd come to my home once a week to do her laundry and mine. Our system helped us both. She didn't have to go to a laundromat, and I came home to clean clothes. There may be ways your family members can help and become a part of your village, even if that doesn't include minding your child while you are away.

Educate your family about your child's disability.

Another way your family can become a more significant part of your support system is if they have a complete understanding of your child's specific challenges and abilities. Invite family members to therapy and doctor appointments, so they get firsthand information. Many of these appointments now have virtual opportunities to attend, so if your family isn't local, inquire with your provider if they can attend these appointments via Zoom or other virtual platforms.

Share articles and pamphlets with them that explain your child's individual needs to help them understand the issues and challenges your family faces. Just knowing you've helped educate your extended family about your child's exceptional needs can help alleviate your stress during family gatherings and conversations. Your family will also understand how to have proper expectations of your child in the same way you do!

Sometimes parents attempt to hide their child's diagnosis from family members. These parents may choose to hide it for fear that they may not receive support or fear that their child may be judged or rejected because of the diagnosis.

Unfortunately, their fears may be valid because these are possible outcomes. Generational gaps, misunderstood stigmas, and fear of the unknown can cause family members not to join your support system right away. If that happens, the only thing you can do is continue to educate them and advocate for your child. Hopefully, with time, they will come around.

You may already receive great support from your family, but I know some families aren't getting any support. Remember, your family members may not know how best to help, so it's up to you to let them know. Be specific in what you ask, continue to educate them, and above all, advocate for your child, even with family.

MAKE IT PERSONAL

Bringing your family into your village was the topic of Chapter 3. Why? Because your family members already unconditionally love you and your child. They may not know how to show it or how to help, but with some guidance, hopefully, you can get them there!

Fill out this chapter's "Make it Personal," date it, and put a note on your calendar to come back and *reflect on your progress in one month.

Today's Date:_____

One Month Later:_____

My Family

How much support (physical or emotional) do you feel you receive from your family currently?

Are they understanding and onboard in accepting your exceptional child's strengths and struggles?

If not, are there things you could do to educate, inform, or enlighten them into a deeper understanding?

Would you like to make some improvements in the support you have from your family, understanding that some of them may not be ready yet to accept the truth that you've had to accept?

Referring back to this chapter's simple suggestions, what are three ways to help bring your family into your village of support?

1. _____
2. _____
3. _____

Reflection: Did the support I receive from my family improve this month?

If not, I am going to let it go. I've done everything I can do. The ball is now in their court.

4

MY VILLAGE INCLUDES
MY FRIENDS WITHIN THE
SPECIAL NEEDS COMMUNITY

*Friendship is the comfort of knowing
that even when you feel alone, you aren't.*
– Author Unknown

In the early days of my son's diagnoses of ADHD and autism, one of the struggles I faced was a feeling of isolation. I did not know anyone who had gone through what I was experiencing. I was scared. I had nothing but unanswered questions, and I felt like I was constantly holding my breath, waiting for those answers that weren't readily available. What was the future going to look like for my child? What would the impact of his diagnosis be on our family? How could I confidently handle the challenges he faced?

I didn't know what was normal anymore. I didn't feel I could relate to other parents of children my son's age. Eventually, I realized I needed to connect with other parents who shared my experience, both to learn from and to lean on.

I took the initiative. Initially, I joined online special needs communities and support groups. Through these groups, I began to see that my life as an exceptional needs parent was normal; it was just a new normal. I saw parents expressing my same doubts and concerns but also an unwavering acceptance. From them, I learned I can be confused and scared and STILL accept and embrace my son's autism. Finally, I felt I could exhale!

I then made friends with a few parents of children who attended therapy with my son. The first time I went to breakfast with one of these parents, we couldn't stop talking. We each appreciated being with someone who understood our unique parenting challenges.

When I spend time with parents within the exceptional needs community, we share our children's difficulties and what we face as their parents. Yet, I still always leave feeling uplifted, optimistic, and hopeful. Even when we can't meet in person, especially during the pandemic, we keep in touch and encourage each other via texting, email, or Zoom. These friends have become the pillars of my support system.

Navigating the world of exceptional needs parenting is overwhelming. The constant decisions we must make about our children regarding such issues as medical care, education, and therapy, can leave us feeling uncertain and constantly doubting that we have made the best decisions. I am grateful that I now have friends who understand these sentiments. When I must make a new decision regarding my child, they are the first people I turn to for advice.

Feeling connected to another person through a similar struggle can help you overcome feelings of isolation. It can help you find a new normal when you realize other families share your unique situation.

I recommend finding two groups of friends within the exceptional needs community. The first group is friends who have a child your child's same age with a similar diagnosis. These are the friends who can relate to everything you are feeling at this moment in time because they are feeling it too.

The second group is friends who have a child with your child's same diagnosis but are a few years older than your child. These friends are your mentors. You can ask them questions and turn to them for advice because they've been where you are.

And one day down the road, you'll more than likely become a mentor for a parent just like you! You'll have the opportunity to give back to a parent who is struggling to find the peace and acceptance you will have discovered!

At first, taking the initiative to seek out these friends might feel awkward, but trust me, they are looking for you, too!

MAKE IT PERSONAL

This chapter's focus was on creating friendships with friends inside the exceptional needs community. Why? Because these are the people who understand firsthand what you are going through. Some are ahead of you on this journey, some at the same place, and some a little behind. But each has an essential role in helping you flesh out your village, and you in helping them flesh out theirs.

Fill out this chapter's "Make it Personal," date it, and put a note on your calendar to come back and *reflect on your progress in one month.

Today's Date:_____

One Month Later:_____

Do you have friends inside the exceptional needs community with children your child's same age and similar diagnosis who understand what you are going through?

Do you have friends inside the exceptional needs community with children a little older than yours with a similar diagnosis who have been where you are and can serve as a mentor?

Do you have friends inside the special needs community with children a little younger than yours with a similar diagnosis that you can support?

Would you like to build more friendships with people within the exceptional needs community?

Referring back to this chapter's simple suggestions, what are three easy ways you can build friendships within the exceptional needs community?

1. _____
2. _____
3. _____

Reflection: Have I made friends within the exceptional needs community during the previous month?

If not, I am going to let it go and try again next month.

5

MY VILLAGE INCLUDES MY FRIENDS OUTSIDE THE SPECIAL NEEDS COMMUNITY

There is only one thing better than making a new friend, and that is keeping an old one.

– Elmer G. Letterman

As important as it is to have friends within the special needs community, you also need other friends. You need a break from being immersed in that space. You need friends you feel a connection with, not because of a similar situation but because you genuinely care for one another.

In Chapter 1, I wrote about the importance of emotional health. I shared that after my son's autism diagnosis, I went through a grieving period. I briefly ended relationships with friends whose children didn't have autism, and I went to counseling. As difficult as that time was, I am grateful I experienced that phase. It opened my eyes to the power of therapy and why I needed those friends in my life.

During that time, those friends reached out and supported me in ways that left me speechless and amazed. Even though they were disappointed that I backed away from our friendships, they sent emails and texts. They told me they wouldn't push me but would be there for me when I was ready.

One of those friends sent me a book by Andrew Solomon, *Far From the Tree: Parents, Children, and the Search for Identity.* Voted by the New York Times as one of the ten best books of 2012, *Far From the Tree* is an intimate examination of more than 300 families of children affected by various exceptional needs and abilities. At its core is the question, "To what extent do we accept our children as they are, and to what extent do we help them become their best selves?"

This book came into my life at one of my lowest points as a mother. I genuinely believe that this book, along with therapy, helped save me from depression. It helped me to realize the answer to the above question is both. I will accept my child for who he is while simultaneously helping him become his best self.

I am thankful for those friends. They acknowledged that even though they didn't understand what I was going through, they still wanted to be a part of my village.

My life shouldn't always be about my son's needs. Sometimes I need to focus on my needs, and you need to focus on yours too. We will always place our children's needs as a high priority, but their needs shouldn't be above our own. And having great friends is one of the best things you can do for yourself.

MAKE IT PERSONAL

This chapter's focus was maintaining friendships outside the exceptional needs community. Why? Because these are the friends who you share a connection with that is personal to you, aside from your child. These are friends you've grown up with, or met in college, or met in other organic ways. These are friends with who you have similar interests and genuine care for one another.

Fill out this chapter's "Make it Personal," date it, and put a note on your calendar to come back and reflect on your progress in one month.*

Today's Date:_____

One Month Later:_____

Friends Outside the Exceptional Needs Community

Can you recall a special memory you had with a close friend before becoming an exceptional needs parent?

How has having a child with exceptional needs impacted previous friendships?

Can you name some friends you were once close to but have drifted apart that you'd like to reconnect with?

Referring back to this chapter's simple suggestions, what are three easy ways to reconnect or maintain relationships with friends outside the exceptional needs community?

1. _____
2. _____
3. _____

Reflection: Have I done anything to reconnect or maintain relationships with friends outside the exceptional needs community in the previous month?

If not, I am going to let it go and try again next month.

6

MY VILLAGE INCLUDES PROFESSIONALS WHO SUPPORT ME

*Learn from the experts; you will not live long
enough to figure it all out by yourself.*
– Brian Tracy

The next "neighborhood" in your village is your professional support system, made up of people who are experts in things you aren't. Your professional support system may include people such as your doctors, therapist, nutritionists, fitness coach, and other types of specialists.

As parents of children with exceptional needs, we often overlook our own health and well-being because so much of our time is devoted to overseeing our child's health and well-being. When was the last time you went to your primary care doctor for a physical and bloodwork? When was the last time you had counseling or therapy? Are you neglecting proper treatment for a health condition that personally affects you?

Many caregivers or parents reading this may have a difficult time answering these questions, including me. I am also guilty of neglecting my health. But our children need us to be as healthy as possible to meet the high demands of caring for them.

My professional support system includes people such as my primary care physician, my good friend who is a fitness coach and motivates me to make healthy life choices, and my therapist. I even include my dentist because she knows the needs of my family and is flexible with us.

Additionally, I include experts I've never met, such as online parenting coaches and ADHD and autism experts. I follow their blogs, YouTube channels, podcasts, and online seminars. I've reached out to several of these experts, asked questions, and received valuable feedback to questions I've had about raising a child with exceptional needs. Any expert or specialist you look to for support and information is someone you can add to this category.

Your professional support system is a crucial part of your village. Your ability to take care of your child depends on how well you take care of yourself. These are the people whose occupation is to do just that. These people have dedicated their lives to helping you, and all you have to do is let them.

MAKE IT PERSONAL

This chapter's focus was on building and taking advantage of your professional support system. Why? Because the professionals that support you help you support your child. They allow you to become the best version of yourself!

Fill out this chapter's "Make it Personal," date it, and put a note on your calendar to come back and reflect on your progress in one month.*

Today's Date:_____

One Month Later:_____

Take a moment to list all the professionals that are a part of your professional support system.

Looking at your list, do you see any gaps? If so, what are they?

When was the last time you reached out to anyone in your professional support system for an appointment or to ask a question?

Is it time to pick up the phone and make some appointments for yourself?

Referring back to this chapter's simple suggestions, what are three easy ways to build and receive support from your professional support system?

1. _____
2. _____
3. _____

Reflection: Have I made progress in building and receiving support from my professional system over the previous month?

If so, how?

If not, I am going to let it go and try again next month.

7

MY VILLAGE INCLUDES PROFESSIONALS WIIO SUPPORT MY CHILD

Where there are experts, there will be no lack of learners.
— Swahili Proverb

In the same way a professional support system is integral to you personally, so is the professional support system for your child. Your child's professional support system includes people such as their pediatrician, developmental pediatrician, therapists, and teachers.

Each time a new situation arises that I feel ill-equipped to handle, I reach out to my son's professional support system. I jokingly refer to exceptional needs parenting as a game of Whack-a-Mole. When a challenge emerges in our family, I take a metaphorical hammer and whack it. That hammer represents things such as research, intervention, and therapy.

It never fails: As soon as we get one challenge under control, a new one rears its head, and we have to whack it. But even though this analogous game of Whack-a-Mole never seems to end, I feel confident that my son's professional support system can help us work through any situation because we are a team.

For example, haircuts used to be a significant challenge for my son. It was sensory overload. He'd immediately become anxious as we pulled up to the salon. Once inside, my husband and I would have to pin his arms and hold his head still for the stylist to cut his hair, as our son screamed throughout the ordeal. It was a horrible experience for everyone.

His behavior therapist, hairstylist, and I worked for months developing a plan. His hairstylist told me to hold an electric toothbrush next to his ears and neck to familiarize him with the clippers' vibration. His behavior therapist told me to make a social story about haircuts and to give him pretend haircuts at home. It took the combined effort of us all, but a year later, he happily walks into the salon. If I hadn't reached out to the experts, he might still have meltdowns during haircuts (or hair past his shoulders)!

Just as in my professional support system, I also have professionals in my son's support system I have never met. I follow their blogs and podcasts to gain new perspectives and keep up to date on the latest research.

My son is only six, but I am learning now what to expect as he approaches school age, then becomes a teenager, and even as he transitions to adulthood. To be successful in this special parenting role, we must meet our children's needs where they are today while at the same time working toward what may lie ahead, knowing that may change.

I know you are busy, but leaning on your child's professional support system can make things easier for you and your child. Pick up the phone and call the doctor the second you see a medication may not be working. Arrange a meeting with your child's teacher if you believe your child is overwhelmed by the assigned amount of homework. Seek out the best bloggers on your child's diagnosis and subscribe, so you have fresh perspectives each day to inspire you.

Your child thrives best when you become an expert in their needs, and reaching out to those who are already experts is one way to work toward that goal.

MAKE IT PERSONAL

This chapter's focus was on building and taking advantage of your child's professional support system. Why? Because the professionals have the expertise and knowledge to help your child in ways you may not.

Fill out this chapter's "Make it Personal," date it, and put a note on your calendar to come back and reflect on your progress in one month.*

Today's Date:_____

One Month Later:_____

Take a moment to list all the professionals that are a part of your child's professional support system.

Looking at your list, do you see any gaps? If so, what are they?

When was the last time you reached out to anyone in your child's professional support system for an appointment or to ask a question?

Is it time to pick up the phone and make some appointments for your child?

Referring back to this chapter's simple suggestions, what are three easy ways to build and receive support from your child's professional support system?

1. _____
2. _____
3. _____

Reflection: Have I made progress in building and receiving support from my child's professional system over the previous month?

If so, how?

If not, I am going to let it go and try again next month.

8

MY VILLAGE INCLUDES NON-PROFIT ORGANIZATIONS

Volunteers do not necessarily have the time;
they just have the heart
— Elizabeth Andrew

The final area to annex to your village to help support you and your child is nonprofit organizations. These organizations include people who are genuinely dedicated and passionate about supporting the exceptional needs community. Before I had my son, I had no idea how many volunteer and nonprofit organizations existed that I could turn to for support.

I found a local university that has an autism center. They provide free parent training on various topics, such as increasing compliance, potty training, and puberty. They also host family events such as special needs community get-togethers at zoos, parks, and libraries.

I turned to another nonprofit when my son needed special education advocacy. The advocate went above and beyond to help my son receive the educational accommodations and services he needed. I will forever be grateful.

Another local organization I discovered offers free monthly respite care for families of special needs children and holds events and activities such as holiday parties and birthday celebrations. My family has received tremendous support from each of these organizations in addition to many others.

You can locate nonprofit organizations at your community, state, and national levels. To start, try searching online for local and national organizations specific to your child's disability. Next, email or call them and ask about their services.

Search online for support groups for your child's disability and set a date to go and participate. Search online for organizations within your community that provide respite care or local events and make plans to attend.

Below is my list of top national non-profit organizations that focus on serving the exceptional needs community, most specifically children and families with intellectual disabilities. In most cases, many of these organizations will also have local community-based chapters.

While this is not a comprehensive list, and you will find more local organizations within your community, these are a great place to start! Call each one and ask, "How can you help my family?" You'll be pleasantly surprised by the support you receive!

Top National Non-Profit Organizations

The Arc

The Arc's mission is to promote and protect the human rights of people with intellectual and developmental disabilities and actively support their full inclusion and participation in the community throughout their lifetimes. The Arc focuses on five core values: people first, equity, community, self-determination, and diversity. Their initiatives encompass criminal justice, education, future planning, employment, health, technology, travel, and volunteering. You can contact The Arc at 1-800-433-5255 and visit their website at **www.thearc.org**.

The Autism Society

The Autism Society is the nation's oldest and largest autism grassroots organization in the United States. From the parent of a newly diagnosed child who doesn't know where to turn to the sibling of an adult on the spectrum who now finds himself in the position of primary caregiver, the Autism Society can help. They assist families in locating resources within their community, such as finding great therapists, schools, or even friends. The Autism Society also has local chapters in most areas.

You can contact The Autism Society at 1-800-328-8476 and visit their website at **www.autismsociety.org**.

Autism Speaks

Autism Speaks' mission is to promote solutions across the spectrum and throughout the lifespan for the needs of individuals with autism and their families through advocacy and support, by increasing understanding and acceptance of people with autism spectrum disorder, and by advancing research into causes and better interventions for autism spectrum disorder and related conditions.

One of their current initiatives, The Next 10, sets goals for the next ten years to foster a better understanding of the causes of ASD, ensure children are diagnosed before age 2, provide access to appropriate intervention upon diagnosis, and make certain that people with ASD have transitions plans and supports in place throughout the adult life.

The Autism Response Team (ART) is a particularly helpful division of Autism Speaks. ART members are trained specifically to help families find information and resources within their community, such as where to get a diagnosis, schools and special education, adult services, and more. You can contact the ART at 1-888-288-4762 and visit Autism Speaks on the web at **www. autismspeaks.org.**

CHADD – Children and Adults with Attention-Deficit/ Hyperactivity Disorder

CHADD (Children and Adults with Attention-Deficit/ Hyperactivity Disorder) was founded in 1987 to help families of those affected with ADHD. CHADD focuses on multiple initiatives such as advocacy, education, and awareness. One of their initiatives, The National Resource Center (NRC), was established to be a national clearinghouse of the latest evidence-based research on ADHD. You can contact CHADD at 1-866-200-8098 or visit their website at **www.chadd.org.**

Collaborative Corner for Exceptional Children

Collaborative Corner is an online resource where families of children with exceptional needs can email questions to a panel of industry experts such as behavior analysts, feeding therapists, mental health counselors, special education advocates, speech therapists, and more. A panelist will respond to the family's questions within 24 hours. Additionally, Collaborative Corner offers Client Concierge, Special Education Advocacy, and other services nationwide. You can contact Collaborative Corner at (401) 217-2702 and visit their website at **www.collaborativecorner.org.**

Easter Seals

Founded in 1919, Easter Seals is America's largest non-profit healthcare organization. They offer resources to more than a million individuals and families living with a disability through a network of 69 local affiliates in communities nationwide, along with four international partners in Australia, Mexico, Puerto Rico, and Canada. Easter Seals offers hundreds of home and community-based services and supports categorized into five distinct support areas: Live, Learn, Work, Play, and Act. You can contact Easter Seals at 1-800-221-6827 or go online to **www.easterseals.com** for more information.

National Autism Association

The mission of the National Autism Association is to respond to the most urgent needs of the autism community, providing real help and hope so all who are affected can reach their full potential. They achieve their mission by addressing initiatives in the following areas: advocacy, research, education, direct tools, thoughtful awareness, and hope. They offer multiple programs, downloadable resources, toolkits, and support through local chapters and groups. You can contact the National Autism Association at 1-877-622-2884 or go online to **www.nationalautismassociation.org** to find resources or to locate your local chapter.

OAR: Organization for Autism Research

OAR's mission is to apply research to the challenges of autism. They use research that directly impacts the quality of life for individuals with autism in areas such as education, communication, self-care, social skills, employment, behavior, and adult and community life. They support multiple initiatives such as *Hire Autism* to help autistic adults find employment, *Operation Autism*, a resource guide for military families, and *Think Safety*, which aims to provide information in keeping individuals with autism safe over the lifespan. You can contact OAR at 1-866-366-9710 or go online to **www.researchautism.org** for additional information.

Special Needs Alliance

The Special Needs Alliance (SNA) is a national organization comprised of attorneys committed to the practice of disability and public benefits law. The SNA's mission is to maintain a professional organization of attorneys skilled in the complex areas of public entitlements, estate, trust and tax planning, and legal issues involving individuals with physical and cognitive disabilities.

Their primary initiative is to connect families with attorneys in their community through a searchable database that understands special needs law complexities.

In addition to helping connect families with a highly qualified special needs attorney, the SNA website also serves as a special needs law information resource. Their website includes information on topics such as:

- Life Care Planning
- Special Needs Trusts
- ABLE accounts
- Special Education
- Government Benefits

Visit at **www.specialneedsalliance.org**.

Special Olympics

The mission of Special Olympics is to provide year-round sports training and athletic competition in a variety of Olympic-type sports for children and adults with intellectual disabilities, giving them continual opportunities to develop physical fitness, demon-strate courage, experience joy, and participate in a sharing of gifts, skills, and friendship with their families, other Special Olympics athletes and the community. They have a wide range of programs and initiatives around the country and internationally. You can contact the Special Olympics at 1-800-700-8585 or visit **www. specialolympics.org**.

United Cerebral Palsy

United Cerebral Palsy (UCP) is an organization dedicated to supporting those with cerebral palsy, intellectual disabilities, and other conditions in living their lives to the fullest. Their initiatives include a resource guide to help families connect with local support services and providers, a Medicaid handbook, and caregiver support. You can contact United Cerebral Palsy at 1-202-776-0406 or via **www.ucp.org**.

MAKE IT PERSONAL

Nonprofit and volunteer organizations exist because they have a passion for helping families like yours and mine to find the resources and support we need at little to no cost. Let's reflect on how these organizations can become a part of your life. Then come back in a month and review your writing from today.

Today's Date:_____

One Month Later:_____

Take a moment to list all the nonprofit and volunteer organizations your family has received support from. (If the answer is zero, we've got work to do!)

What nonprofit and volunteer organizations that serve families with exceptional needs, besides those listed in this chapter, are you currently aware of?

Have you ever reached out for support or taken advantage of the service any of the organizations mentioned in this chapter offer?

Which organizations in this chapter do you believe could meet the needs of your family? If you listed any, check out their website and look at their services?

Referring back to this chapter's simple suggestions, list three easy ways to build and receive support from nonprofit and volunteer organizations.

_____
_____
_____

Reflection: Have I made progress in building and receiving support from nonprofit and volunteer organizations over the previous month?

If so, how?

If not, I am going to let it go and try again next month.

FINAL THOUGHTS

The village is a place where you can find peace, unity, strength, inspiration, and, most importantly, a natural and beautiful life.
— Minahil Urfan

I have been where you are. It is tough. It is isolating. It is all-consuming. We love our kiddos, but parenting them can be as draining as it is rewarding. I am so honored that you found this book. I am humbled to be a small part of hopefully helping you to build a support system.

By reading this book, you have taken a big step toward creating the support system you, your child, and your family may desperately need. I hope you feel empowered to take the initiative to build a support system if you don't currently have one or strengthen the one you have already built.

Regardless, I am here for you. I know, and I understand what you are going through. I am part of your village.

You've got this!

Amy

RESOURCES

Here you'll find a list of some of my favorite resources listed in the book and a few new ones!

Able Eyes

For families impacted by disabilities, both physical and cognitive, accessing the community can be difficult when not knowing what to expect. Able Eyes, founded Meegan Winters, is a database of virtual tours of businesses throughout the country. At no charge, families can log into Able Eyes, type in the zip code of where they live or where they may be traveling, and virtually tour spaces before arriving.

www.ableeyes.org

Big Abilities Blog & Podcast

The Big Abilities blog & podcast, run by Amy Nielsen, is full of resources, interviews with experts, and practical advice from a mother who understands the unique parenting journey of having a child with exceptional needs. You can find both the blog and podcast at www.bigabilities.com or wherever you listen to podcasts.

Child Senior Safety

Equally important as creating an organized and decluttered home, is making sure your home is safe. Bob Dane of Child Senior Safety has been in the home safety business for over 15 years. Bob's expertise is helping families create safe spaces. His specialty is banister safety walls for exposed lofts. He works with families nationwide.

www.childseniorsafety.com

Collaborative Corner for Exceptional Children

Founded by exceptional needs parent Jessica Barisano, Collaborative Corner is run by a team of industry experts in a wide variety of specialties. Collaborative Corner is an excellent resource for credible resources and information. Their blog, Facebook, and Instagram are valuable tools for families covering a wide range of topics.

www.collaborativecorner.org

Designing Interiors for Autism

When interior designer Wendy Valente's daughter was diagnosed with autism, she found that creating a sensory space for her daughter helped her overcome some of her challenges. Realizing this type of interior design wasn't available at a residential level, Wendy started Designing Interiors for Autism, a niche within her full-service interior design business, Live Well Designs.

www.livewelldesigns.net

Take a Break Babysitting Service

Board Certified Behavior Analyst, Jessica Andrews, founded *Take a Break Behavioral Babysitting* to offer families of children with exceptional needs access to exceptional babysitters and nannies. *Take a Break* is a full-service respite service with highly trained staff offering services such as:

- Full-time nannies
- Hourly babysitters
- After school care
- Travel/vacation services
- Part-time nannies
- Overnight care
- Event sitting
- Mother's helper

www.takeabreaktampa.com

REFERENCES

Brody, Jane E. 2017. "Social Interaction is Critical for Physical and Mental Health." New York Times: June 12, 2017. https://www.nytimes.com/2017/06/12/well/live/having-friends-is-good-for-you.html.

Brown, Mary K. 1992. *Sally's Room.* New York: Scholastic.

Casazza, Allie. 2017. "Declutter Like a Mother." https://alliecasazza.com.

Geary, Ali. 2014. "Eight Simple Steps to Increase Your Intellectual Wellness." Illinois State University. March 26, 2014. https://news.illinoisstate.edu/2014/03/seven-simple-steps-increase-intellectual-wellness.

Kondo, Marie. 2014. *The Life-Changing Magic of Tidying Up.* Berkeley: Ten Speed Press.

Lamothe, Cindy. 2019. "How to Build Good Emotional Health." Healthline. June 14, 2019. https://www.healthline.com/health/emotional-health.

Meltzer, Lisa J. 2008. "Brief Report: Sleep in Parents of Children with Autism Spectrum Disorders." *Journal of Pediatric Psychology* 33 (4): 380-386. https://academic.oup.com/jpepsy/article/33/4/380/1746689.

Psychology Today. n.d. "Spirituality." Psychology Today. Accessed May 9, 2021. https://www.psychologytoday.com/us/basics/spirituality.

Prince, Renee. 2021. "Challenging Ways Technology Affects Your Sleep." Sleep.org. March 12, 2021. https://www.sleep.org/articles/ways-technology-affects-sleep.

SCL Health. n.d. "Why It's Time to Ditch the Phone Before Bed." SCLHealth.org. Accessed May 1, 2021. https://www.sclhealth.org/blog/2019/09/why-it-is-time-to-ditch-the-phone-before bed/#:~:text=The%20National%20Sleep%20Foundation%20recommends,and%20start%20reading%20before%20bed.

Whitbourne, Susan. 2017. "5 Reasons Why Clutter Disrupts Mental Health." Psychology Today. May 13, 2017. https://www.psychologytoday.com/us/blog/fulfillment-any-age/201705/5-reasons-clear-the-clutter-out-your-life.

Watson, Stephanie, and Kristeen Cherney. 2019. "The Effects of Sleep Deprivation on Your Body." Healthline. May 15, 2020. https://www.healthline.com/health/sleep-deprivation/effects-on-body.

ACKNOWLEDGEMENTS

We must find time to stop and thank the people
who make a difference in our lives.
– John F. Kennedy

I want to start by thanking my husband, Brent. His consistent encouragement gave me the confidence to start the Big Abilities blog and podcast, and to start AND finish this book. Even in the middle of a Canucks, Niners, or Jays game, he always stops what he's doing and gives me his undivided attention.

I also want to thank my team of friends and family who eagerly helped me with this book. First is my friend and self-care expert, Bethanne. Thanks, Asset Queen!

My go-to guru for all things clean and tidy is my sister, Abby. She's the only person I know who gets more excited about organizational tools and cleaning tips than I do! Thanks, Abby, for sharing your time and expertise.

My father, Steve, and my mother, Debbie, provided help and suggestions and are in my top tier of support. I appreciate them immensely. Thanks so much, Mom and Dad!

My good friend, Rachel, and some other great friends were there when I went through some tough times. Thanks, Rachel, for your feedback and even more so for your friendship.

Shirleyann is not only the mother of a child with exceptional needs, but she also has her own medical challenges. Her suggestions for the book were invaluable.

Thank you to my eldest daughter, Danielle, an attorney who practices special needs law and contributed to the resources listed in the book.

Also, thank you to my youngest daughter, Olivia, for cracking jokes, making me laugh, and adding some needed humor to my writing process.

I also want to give Chalene Johnson and the PodSquad a shout-out for convincing me this book was possible and for all the support.

Finally, I want to thank my son, Barclay. When you came along, you gave me a new point of view. *You* have helped *me* become a better person. I was never supposed to change you; it was you who was supposed to change me. And you certainly did! You gave me a new purpose in life, to help other parents like me, blessed to have kids like you, find their peace.

ABOUT THE AUTHOR

It is my hope to help my son burst through the ceiling of his disabilities into the universe of his abilities.

– Amy Nielsen

Amy Nielsen spent nearly 20 amazing years as an elementary and middle school educator, working as a media specialist and teaching television production. She is the mother of four children ranging in age from 6-33. Her youngest son has ADHD and Autism Spectrum Disorder. She is the owner of the Big Abilities blog and podcast. In addition to writing her own blog, she does freelance writing for Playground Magazine and has had articles featured on The Mighty, National Autism Resources, Autism Parenting Magazine, Exceptional Needs Today, and more. Most recently, Amy joined the nonprofit organization Collaborative Corner for Exceptional Children, where she serves as Client Concierge Manager and Parent Advocate. Her primary role is to help families find credible resources and quality providers. She hopes to help families who have a child with exceptional needs to not only work on helping their child overcome their struggles but also to focus on building up their strengths. She and her family live in Orlando, Florida.

Made in United States
North Haven, CT
19 February 2022

16259332R00055